A VOICE THROUGH CHOICE

Stories about independent advocacy

Contents

6

Introduction

We are proud to present the first collection of stories about how the Scottish independent advocacy movement has enabled people to have a say, make decisions and take some control of their lives. This book is full of the experiences of real people who have accessed advocacy and it will give the reader an insight into the potential impact advocacy has on all our lives.

This book is the result of many discussions and has been produced to provide an overview of the different types of independent advocacy and introduce the reader to the variety of people who use advocacy in Scotland today. Everyone in the Scottish advocacy movement had an opportunity to make a contribution to this book and we were overwhelmed with the number of responses we received and the generosity of the individuals who gave up their time to tell us about their lives and in particular those who have shared some very difficult experiences with us. Without each of these individuals this book would not have been possible.

There is very little research on how advocacy benefits people and communities and the book is a step towards demonstrating 'advocacy successes' to a wider audience, including people who may benefit from advocacy, funders and people who come into contact with advocacy through their work. The book is also a valuable tool through which to illustrate how the different types of advocacy operate. This book is part of a larger awareness raising project that includes the DVD *Independent Advocacy – A Voice to Trust.*

We want people to read this book and feel inspired to become an advocate, whether that's involved formally with an advocacy organisation or actively advocating for people or a cause they feel passionate about.

We also want Health Boards, Local Authorities and grant giving bodies to read this book to understand how important advocacy is, appreciate the difference it makes and then go ahead and commission and fund it.

" If you want to know something about people's activities, the best way of finding out is to ask them "

- Brenner et al 1985

What is independent advocacy?

Independent advocacy is about standing up to injustice.

Many of us find it difficult, at times, to get our voice heard about decisions or actions that affect our lives. Some people have family, friends or carers to help them to speak up. Some don't have anyone in their lives to help them. Sometimes a family member may have their own ideas about what would be best for the person, which might not be the same as what the person wants. Carers and professionals have a 'duty of care' for the person, which may conflict with their wishes.

Independent advocacy aims to help people by supporting them to express their own needs and make their own informed decisions. Independent advocates support people to gain access to information and explore and understand the options available to them.

The Scottish Independent Advocacy Alliance (SIAA)

The SIAA is a membership organisation responsible for promoting, supporting and defending independent advocacy in Scotland. It has the overall aim of ensuring that independent advocacy is available to any vulnerable person in Scotland.

The SIAA provides information and support, represents advocacy organisations at various levels and raises awareness and understanding of independent advocacy across Scotland. The SIAA works to influence legislation, policy and practice in relation to advocacy.

To find out about advocacy organisations in your area, visit our directory at www.siaa.org.uk

How did we collect the stories in the book?

We used several techniques to gather people's stories:

Story writing

People who wanted to be involved could write their story down as they chose without a guide. This meant that they could write as much or as little as they wanted, in their own words.

Questionnaire

Answering a questionnaire.

Interview

We set up semi-structured interviews. We were keen that the interviews were as 'unstructured' as possible to allow people to talk about their experiences in the way that they wanted to.

Some people chose instead to provide us with poems, quotes and even songs they have written about advocacy.

Members of Advocating Together Self Advocacy Group telling us their stories

We had to make sure that everyone interviewed for the book was treated with respect and dignity and that we used the information people gave us in a way that they wanted us to. Contributors have all had full control over what they shared with us.

Where advocacy partners came forward to be interviewed, most were met with their advocate, at a location convenient to them. This was, in part, to give people confidence and reassurance and to ensure that as researchers, we did not exploit our position working with potentially vulnerable people. Equally, there were always two researchers, this ensured that the story we wrote following the interview was as accurate as possible. Everyone involved in the book volunteered and no financial reward was given for stories.

Everyone was told how their story would be used and why we were producing a book on advocacy. Everyone in the book has given their written consent.

At the beginning of the interview we explained that people could speak as freely as they wanted, in confidence, and that they would be given the opportunity to withdraw anything they didn't want to be used. After the interview we sent a written copy to contributors, explaining that they could edit the information as they wished, or retract their story completely.

Everyone was given a choice of a pseudonym so that they and those they mentioned could not be identified, whilst some chose this option, others were happy to keep their real names. All third party names have been changed, and where appropriate, the location and name of the advocacy organisation has also been changed.

Citizen advocacy

Citizen advocacy happens when ordinary citizens are encouraged to become involved with a person who might need support in their communities. The citizen advocate is not paid and not motivated by personal gain. The relationship between the citizen advocate and their advocacy partner is on a one-to-one, long term basis. The relationship is based on trust between the partner and the advocate and is supported by but not influenced by the advocacy organisation. The advocate will support their partner using their natural skills and talents rather than being trained in the role.

Collective or Group

Collective advocacy is where a group of people who are all facing a common problem get together on a formal basis to support each other over specific issues. Individual members of the group may support each other over specific issues. The group as a whole may campaign on an issue that affects them all. A collective voice can be stronger than that of an individual, groups are more difficult to ignore. Being part of a collective advocacy group can help to reduce an individual's sense of isolation when raising a difficult issue.

Peer advocacy

Peer advocacy is about individuals who share significant life experiences. The peer advocate and their advocacy partner may share age, gender, ethnicity, diagnosis or issues. Peer advocates use their own experiences to understand and empathise with their advocacy partner. Peer advocacy works to increase self awareness, confidence and assertiveness so that the individual can speak out for themselves, lessening the imbalance of power between the advocate and their advocacy partner.

Professional advocacy

Professional advocacy is also known as one to one, individual or issue based advocacy. It is provided by both paid and unpaid advocates. An advocate supports an individual to represent their own interests or represents the views of an individual if the person is unable to do this themselves. They provide support on specific issues and provide information but not advice. This support can be short or long term.

Who is advocacy for...

..."I would recommend advocacy to anyone, any age, because it will help them with any issues that are on their minds."

Billy

What does advocacy mean to you?

... "the world."

Irene

Why advocate...

..."I get great satisfaction from each one of the young people I work with through supporting their voice to be heard and to speak up."

Lorraine Herschell - Partners in Advocacy, Edinburgh

Peter _{and} Jean

Peter and Jean have been in an advocacy partnership for 11 years. Peter first came into contact with advocacy after he was diagnosed with Korsakoffs Psychosis. His diagnosis meant that at the age of 42 he was kept against his will in a care home for older people. Here, he spent 4 years of his life whilst he battled, together with Jean, for a more suitable care package for someone of his age.

Korsakoffs Psychosis is a degenerative form of dementia that can often be caused by chronic alcohol abuse. One of its symptoms is severe short term memory loss. Little is known about the condition and many people who suffer from Korsakoffs are detained because they are considered a danger to themselves...

...This is what happened to Peter...

23

...For 4 years he lived what he describes as a 'living death', confined to four walls, not allowed to go out unsupervised, having to ask to go to the toilet, being washed, rather than washing himself. Through all of this, he was prescribed extremely heavy medication that slowly made him complacent about his situation and made him lose all confidence in his ability to lead a normal life. The drugs often induced him into a stupor, leaving him unable to communicate what he wanted in meetings with staff.

Peter met Jean whilst being treated in hospital, before his move to the care home. The first battle that Peter and Jean faced was trying to convince Social Work that, with the aid of a suitable care package, Peter was a young, able bodied man who had the ability to live by himself. There was, inevitably, an element of risk involved in this decision, and the Social work Department which have a duty of care for Peter, were apprehensive due to the considerable safety implications. But for Peter, the benefits of living in his own space far outweighed the risks. Social Workers felt that left to his own devices, Peter might start to drink again, risking an early death. In Peter's opinion, a short life was worth more than the 'living death'.

...There were also other concerns surrounding Peter's short term memory loss...

...What if he forgot to look before crossing the road and got run over..?

...Not a great deal is known about Korsakoffs and care staff and Jean were learning from Peter as time went on. Peter can speak German and French and understand Latin, so it's clear that not all parts of his memory are affected. He found that looking before he crossed the road was such a natural thing to do, he would not forget.

Peter wanted to live somewhere he had lived before, somewhere that was present in his long term memory. Social Work developed lots of tests to see if Peter could live independently. Could he get from A to B without forgetting where he was going? Could he turn on the stove and remember to turn it off?

Peter has now lived independently in his own flat for 8 years. He has a number of care workers that come and help him, but since Peter's confidence and ability have grown over the years, the hours of care he receives have been greatly reduced. He's devised routines to tackle his confusion, like always writing notes in his wallet and asking everyone to write in his diary to remind him where he was and where he needs to go. Getting Peter out of the care home and arranging a care package were not the only things that Jean helped Peter with...

...Once Peter was in his flat he had another battle to face...

...gaining power of attorney over his finances. When he was first diagnosed with Korsakoffs, he passed all control of his finances to solicitors.

Once Peter felt that he was able to manage his own banking and wanted power of attorney over his own money, the solicitors refused to cooperate. They threatened that if he persisted, they would find a way for him to be put back into hospital. This was a huge and terrifying threat after Peter had worked so hard and been so determined to live independently. The solicitors would send Peter a certain amount of his own money a week but if he wanted something extra, like a new jumper, he would have to write and ask them for more of his own money!

Sometimes, he would ask for £40 and they would write back, saying "we think you only need £30", and Peter would write again, saying that he would like £40 - after all, it was his money. The solicitors would then send him £30 and an invoice charging him for the correspondence. The fight for power over his own money took place over many years. Eventually Jean and Peter took the case to the Legal Services Agency and Peter now has control over his own money and an arrangement with the bank so that he can go in everyday to get a set amount...

...Peter feels that it is thanks to Jean, her determination and hard work, that he is alive today and living such a fulfilling life. He says that without her, he would never have been able to leave the care home or regain control over his finances...

...Through his relationship with Jean and the changes that were made to his life, Peter's flamboyant personality has been able to emerge...

...When Jean first met Peter, his personality was quashed by sterile institutions, depression and heavy medication. Jean watched as Peter slowly put more and more time and effort into decorating his new flat, so that it is now a true reflection of him, a stark contrast to the bare four walls that he had become accustomed to inside institutions...

...As a volunteer advocate, Jean put a lot of work into helping Peter, yet she maintains that she's got back just as much, going on a journey with Peter, meeting people she would never have met and learning so much.

Nowadays, Peter occasionally phones Jean at the office to catch up and Jean sometimes attends meetings with Peter, but by and large Peter leads an ordinary life, or maybe better described as an extraordinary life for someone with Korsakoffs.

Kirsty

Kirsty learnt about advocacy through her school and local visits from an FBS advocacy worker. The advocacy issue was the transition period, as she moved on from school.

Kirsty was very adamant that she did not want to go to her local college. She had been on a link placement with school and didn't like it. She described it as boring and full of people that annoyed her. She wanted to pursue work either in a nursery or a sports centre.

At her leavers meeting her advocate supported her to tell people what she wanted. They all said she should 'just go to college'. They said she couldn't do childcare due to complex qualifications and she would have trouble getting a job. She should 'just go to college'.

The advocate asked about Kirsty's personal learning plan for leaving school. The school said there wasn't one. The advocate asked "careers" if there were any options that could enable Kirsty to work rather than go to college. The careers advisor thought not but agreed to help look.

However they didn't get in contact. The advocate phoned, and phoned. Kirsty was finally given a placement. It didn't work out and the agency disappeared. Kirsty wasn't happy and was advised 'just to go to college'.

Which she did do. However, she did keep on telling people that it wasn't what she wanted to do. With support, she continued to raise this concern. Her mum and the advocate worked together to chase up a Social Work assessment for Kirsty to see if she was entitled to any support, which she was. She is now receiving support two days per week so that she can visit the gym independently without having to go with her mum.

Then Kirsty was referred to another supported employment agency that had expanded their services. She is now working with them and developing her employment profile before having her first work trial.

It is now almost one year since Kirsty left school. The skills that she has learnt from her advocate and those who have supported her have been invaluable in helping her take control of her own life and steer it away from the direction that everyone else seemed to think she should go in. She is now really happy and her confidence continues to grow.

DAVID

Powerful Partnerships provides citizen advocacy for people labelled as having a learning disability, including people who reside within NHS Learning Disability Services.

David is a project worker for Powerful Partnerships. This involves finding ordinary members of the public who want to become citizen advocates, promoting the benefits of independent advocacy to external agencies and finding people with learning disabilities, who may want a citizen advocate.

" I came to advocacy after having worked as a personal care assistant, where I had regular contact with advocates from a range of organisations. I became further interested in the field whilst attending a part-time psychotherapy training course, where I heard about the principles and functions of citizen advocacy from one of my fellow trainees.

A lasting citizen advocacy partnership provides a person at risk of being marginalised or excluded from society with someone who will stand alongside them, either in times of difficulty or when trying to branch out and make friends in the community. A citizen advocate is independent of any external pressure or influence, whether that be from family, health and social care professionals or paid support staff. In situations where family members die, or paid workers move on, for instance, a citizen advocate will be the source of continuous support and companionship to help their partner through the transition and plan for the future.

Citizen advocacy is also a way of kick-starting friendships; friendships that, if left to chance, might never have developed due to the continued segregation of people with disabilities from the rest of society. This could be due to the institutionalised lives of many service users, the inaccessibility of public facilities and social/cultural venues, and/or lack of awareness amongst members of the public that such people exist and might need our support and companionship.

Many of the qualities of a citizen advocate are those that I would expect from a soul mate or close friend: patience, open-mindedness, determination, empathy, dependability, optimism, honesty and sincerity - to name but a few.

At times, as a project worker, it can be very frustrating when I struggle to find a suitable potential advocate for someone referred to me - perhaps on an urgent basis - especially when a lot of effort has gone into networking, advertising, personal approaches, talks and presentations. All the while, I am aware that the person referred is not receiving the citizen advocate they so badly need.

,,

Natalie and Rachel

Natalie has been a citizen advocate for Rachel for four years. Rachel has cerebral palsy, she is now 21 and lives in a residential care home. They have a friendship based partnership and Natalie now sees Rachel as part of her family. She has such a commitment to Rachel that if something were to happen to her, Natalie's family would take over her role and look out for Rachel.

A voluntary organisation Natalie was volunteering for recommended her to the citizen advocacy project as someone who would be a good citizen advocate. The special needs school that Rachel attended referred Rachel to the project as someone who would benefit from advocacy. They were matched together by the project because they were a similar age and had similar social interests. In addition, Natalie had an open attitude to all types of disability and knew Rachel from work that she had done at the school previously.

Although each citizen advocate is different and each partnership varies, the views of a citizen advocate are generally that you look out for your advocacy partner like you would for a friend or neighbour. It is not something that you put on your CV, or say is a piece of voluntary work. You don't earn a wage and no expenses are paid. In return, the experiences you gain are invaluable. Although Rachel may not communicate in a way that most people are familiar with, Natalie says that she has gained and learnt just as much from Rachel as Natalie has given...

...The basis of a citizen advocacy partnership is that you develop a very long term relationship with a vulnerable member of your community and all the boundaries that apply to independent professional advocacy can be lost. So, in effect the person can become like another member of your family or a friend...

This is true of Natalie and Rachel, they see each other every week and at times Natalie has been the only significant person in Rachel's life. Like a family member would do, Natalie spends time with Rachel, the time that is needed to get to know her sounds, her movements, her likes, her dislikes and her moods.

She has an understanding of her personality; a privilege that many health professionals never have due to the time restraints in their job. It is this lack of understanding that can leave Rachel vulnerable to decisions and misunderstandings made about her care and needs. Like a family member would be, Natalie is there to draw attention to certain things that need to be addressed in Rachel's care. In this way, the role of the advocate is of great value...

...Rachel will never understand the concept that her family doesn't visit her, but the fact that Natalie visits her counts for just as much.

"

"Injustice anywhere is a threat to justice everywhere."

Martin Luther King Jr.

SAGE

Senior Action Group Edinburgh

collective advocacy in care homes for the elderly

" Our group started when residents from care homes saw the need for a collective advocacy group where they could have a voice. We have looked at various issues over the years. These have included communal living, nutrition in care homes, care standards, care practice, planning new care homes, diversity issues, staffing, security checks on staff, activities, boredom in the care home, responding to Government consultations, and generally being involved in various older people's strategies across the city.

Our main aim is to make a positive change to care practice by giving residents a clear voice but we have also influenced policy and practice at national and local levels. For example, we have petitioned the Scottish Parliament regarding the amount of personal allowance paid to residents in care homes. We also work with service providers and other stakeholders to make sure that older people are fully involved in the democratic decision making process.

"It's fabulous to know you're not alone."

The groups take time and commitment. The changes we are trying to make are for the long term. There is no point in joining a group and then leaving because you did not get the result you wanted. The same issues arise again and again. We just find new ways of dealing with them. You have to work closely with other people in the same arena. Eventually someone hears you. It is important that the groups can work together for the common cause. There is no room for large egos in our work! Who would have thought that older people living in care homes would be part of the design team for the new care home at Lochend. We did! Change can happen but it takes time.

"

"Before SAGE I felt my life was not whole. They have given me a new lease of life."

"I enjoy meeting the groups. We get together and discuss issues that are happening in the care homes. We try to make things better."

Advocacy is...

..."Supporting folk along their journey and walking beside them for at least a while."

Ivan Barry, advocate,
Circles Network Advocacy Project,
based in the Royal Edinburgh Hospital

Ruth_{and} Devrim

Ruth first found out about advocacy whilst a patient in the Royal Edinburgh Hospital. At first, Ruth was suspicious of people that she came into contact with, as her past experiences had led her to believe that her views and wishes were often ignored or dismissed. She felt isolated, with people unwilling to listen to her and she found it difficult to get her views across.

RUTH

After using Circles Network Advocacy Project, a hospital-based advocacy organisation, when she left the Royal Edinburgh she was passed onto AdvoCard, a similar organisation for those in the community. Through her relationship with Devrim, her advocacy worker at AdvoCard, Ruth was able to see that there was someone on her side and at meetings with psychiatrists, clinicians or others she felt that she was able to speak up for herself because Devrim was present.

Ruth also feels that having an advocate with you can change the way that you are treated or spoken to by professional bodies. Having Devrim there made Ruth feel that there was a witness to what was said and done. After meetings Devrim would type up minutes, which enabled Ruth to look back at what was said.

Over time Ruth's confidence grew and Devrim suggested that she might consider becoming a volunteer advocacy worker. Last year Ruth completed AdvoCard's volunteer advocacy training programme and now advocates for other people.

When Ruth first came across the idea of advocacy, she could not have imagined that she would be advocating for others. Ruth is also involved in advocacy in other ways, as a member of the AdvoCard Management Committee. Through this she has received useful training on a variety of topics.

Ruth recognises that advocacy can help people and empower them to make changes in their life. Her experience as an inpatient on a psychiatric ward was a real 'eye opener'. This is what motivated her to become involved in some way.

DEVRIM

Devrim works as an independent advocate for AdvoCard, providing advocacy for people subject to the Mental Health Act*. This can involve preparing for tribunals and helping to write Advance Statements.

He finds working one to one with people particularly enjoyable and after working in the care and social sector, and witnessing how many people get treated, he finds advocacy very satisfying.

* Mental Health (Care and Treatment) (Scotland) Act 2003

JOHN

John works for Advocacy Matters, Greater Glasgow which provides independent professional advocacy for adults over the age of 16 who have mental health problems. He has been involved in advocacy for just over three years.

" I had given up a career in IT in the 90's to pursue a dream of going to Art College. After graduating, I realised that I'd never make a living from my work so I decided that if I had to work, I wanted to do something 'ethical'. I started from the bottom, as a support worker in a mental health project in Dundee. After two years I realised that I was under used and had more to offer. So I decided to move into independent advocacy. This was at a very interesting time when organisations were gearing up for the Mental Health (Care and Treatment) (Scotland) Act 2003.

45

The best thing about independent advocacy is working one to one with people who previously were disempowered and joining them on the journey to empowerment and hopefully recovery. Sometimes this takes dramatic forms but mostly it is prosaic, with people satisfied that they are being listened to and that someone is taking an interest in them.

Despite this, it can be frustrating that our work involves a lot of responsibility but we have no authority. We also spend all day working on peoples' problems, and no one ever calls to pass the time of day or say everything is fine. This can sometimes make maintaining the qualities of an advocacy worker: empathy, understanding, a supportive attitude, a struggle.

Without being egotistical, advocates are minor unsung heroes. Much of the work we do is invisible to anyone but our advocacy partners. I feel privileged that so many people allow us into their lives despite the difficulties they face engaging with service providers. I would like to think that should I become ill, I would find an independent advocate to support me.

Advocacy is a job where experience is rated as much as qualifications. ,,

"Seeing people who have felt disempowered and misrepresented gain confidence and take control of their lives. Previous partners have become members of our Board of Directors, who have become my employers. That's about as good as it gets."

Linda Coates - Advocacy Matters, Greater Glasgow

Released from Prison
with nowhere to go

" Anthony came to our office one winter's Friday afternoon, about one hour after we had received a phone message from Criminal Justice Social Work at the local prison. The message informed us that Anthony had been released and had been told that he could access help from our advocacy service. We were given no further information, although Anthony had previously approached our service for support with a housing issue, and was therefore known to us, at least superficially. During that previous involvement Anthony had expressed concerns that he was not receiving any help with his mental health issues. He had not followed up appointments we had helped him to arrange, had drifted out of contact with us and had also ended up back in prison, having been found guilty of breach of the peace and shoplifting charges.

Sure enough, Anthony turned up at our office at 3pm on the Friday afternoon, with many urgent needs. He was having serious difficulties sorting these out because he was prevented by interdict from attending the local housing, benefits, Social Work and Criminal Justice offices. These interdicts were based on the grounds that Anthony represented a threat to females, through his intimidating and aggressive behaviour. No mention of these facts was made to us by the referring Social Worker, and we were fortunate that I was in the office (I am male) as well as our (female) office manager. He therefore had very little cash, no way of accessing benefits, no accommodation, no Social Work support, and no food. He was still adamant that he was affected by mental health problems, but had received no support in prison, nor referral to GP or other services upon his discharge. He was still adamant that he was affected by psychotic illness, and declared that he had twice been "sectioned" in the past, although not in our area.

As I attempted to access services for Anthony, it became apparent from responses that he was not allowed access to any of the services he needed because of the perceived threat he posed...

...The irony of this situation was not lost on us, as the very service (criminal justice) who had referred him to us, without warning and without concern for our female staff, were denying him their own support, even though their own offices and reception are protected by strengthened glass and security systems...

Nevertheless, we
found Anthony to be
calm and polite...

...and through a series of assertive phone calls and discussions, were able to secure Anthony emergency accommodation for the weekend, a food parcel from another voluntary organisation, and an appointment with myself for the Monday morning.

Anthony kept this appointment and turned up on time, homeless again, but more concerned about his unaddressed mental health issues, the danger he felt he posed to females as a result of his anger and his fear that he would have to "do something else" in order to get sent back to prison, if he could not find accommodation or benefits...

...He was polite, courteous and we did not feel under threat from him. I was, however, aware that he was anxious and uncertain about his future...

...We were unable to organise appointments with any of the statutory services because of the interdicts, and neither would those services accept a visit from him with myself accompanying him. The Benefits Agency agreed to post him an emergency payment but as he had no address asked if they could use our address for him, and post him a giro which he could pick up from our office. Mental health services were equally reluctant to accept a referral from us.

Inevitably, Anthony spent two more nights sleeping rough, without supervision and we next met him after he had spent another short while in detention for breach of the peace. He came back to our offices immediately after his release, in the same situation, having been denied access to the benefits office. It was at this point that I suggested that he actually contact the police to request that they accompany him to benefits and housing offices.

Although initially surprised at the idea, Anthony agreed to give it a go. It had never occurred to him (or to me!) that the police could actually help him. After negotiating these arrangements, Anthony then did manage to access those services, and I was able to write to mental health services, requesting an assessment from the Community Mental Health Team...

...Anthony kept these appointments, and although he never returned formally to our service (we had no way of contacting him) I did meet him in the street about one month later, and he had been successful in getting a one bedroom flat in town and some support from mental health services. He was better dressed, more relaxed, and a little more confident that he would not need to return to prison...

...During the process of helping Anthony, we were able to confirm that he had in fact been a patient in mental health wards on two previous occasions. Social Workers argued that he was affected by a personality disorder, whilst Anthony was adamant that he suffered from mental illness. Although services stressed the level of danger that they felt Anthony posed to their staff, he did not have any convictions for violence. They did not seem to consider that denying him access to their services put both Anthony, the public (as he slept rough) or the voluntary sector (ourselves) at risk. This created a cycle whereby Anthony's only recourse in cold, homeless December, was to re-offend and thereby re-enter the shelter and security of prison, despite the risks implicit in that cycle...

...We never felt under any threat from Anthony, and although he expressed his own anger, fear and frustration as he explained his situation to us, he seemed to genuinely accept that we were committed to helping him and advocating for his needs...

...Anthony stays in my memory because his plight is so illustrative of so many vulnerable, single men, whose mental health problems are more conveniently described as "personality disorder".

The corollary is that society and services then "process" thousands of Anthonys as "criminal" despite their appeals for mental health support. The increasing cycle of petty criminality distances mental health services from a potential client, and antagonises Anthony towards Criminal Justice, Social Work and housing. Those services then feel threatened, and each turning of the cycle ratchets up the tension, so that the potential for a more serious offence increases. At one point, Anthony said to me that unless he got the help he needed, he might have to really hurt someone, so that at least he would not have to keep leaving prison.

I am not saying that Anthony had never done anything of a criminal nature or that he was not at least in part responsible for his situation. I have now lost touch completely with him and hope that if he reads this story and recognises himself in it that he will remember our help as genuine and non-judgemental. This case emphasised to me how individuals fall between stools and enter terrifying freefall into negative spirals.

All other services had abandoned or antagonised Anthony, yet we found him to be frightened, courteous and non-threatening. His story showed me, yet again, the value of advocacy in very demanding situations. Although we did not solve all his problems, we were able to help him be heard and begin to rebuild a life. His interactions with us, and ours with other services, also showed up how imperfect and unreliable their communications can be and gave us the impetus to begin negotiating better referrals to advocacy within prison and criminal justice systems.

I believe that because we genuinely listened to Anthony, and worked openly with him to help him be heard, we did not feel threatened by him, nor did he feel antagonistic towards us. It is often the case that the voluntary sector (let's not forget that food parcel) provides the real help when it matters."

Steve

"Initially I wanted to go into teaching and to be honest I just wanted something for my CV, but now, this is what I do on a Tuesday, it's part of my life and I can't imagine life without it. I've even got a paid job with another advocacy organisation!

I'm a volunteer self advocacy assistant for a group of people with learning disabilities. There are about 10 people in my group along with other volunteers who also support the group...

...Every Tuesday we meet up and do something different, sometimes we'll have a chat and drink cups of tea, other times a group member might have a specific issue that they want to talk about...

...Occasionally people from Social Work, the Local Authority or Health Board come and consult the group, asking them what they think about a document that is going to be published or a development that is being built.

What's really good is that the group are really supportive of one another, they all help one another with day to day problems. For example, one person came to the group with troubles they were having with the building work in their flat, and it turned out that others had experienced similar problems, so they helped the person to sort it out.

In a self advocacy group the members support each other by sharing knowledge and experiences and they build up their confidence in order to advocate for themselves. Part of my role as a self advocacy assistant is to offer practical support, and help to find information. Once, a person close to a member of the group was taken into hospital and nobody told them where the person had gone or when they could visit. I helped the member to find out who the contact at the hospital was and the contact details for the hospital, so that they could make the call themselves...

...Working with people with learning disabilities has opened my eyes. I've really learnt a lot about my own prejudices, and sometimes I think 'you can't do that, can you?' Everyone in the group is different and has different ways of communicating and different skills and abilities. ,,

Why fund advocacy?

Lynda Thompson,
Commissioner, NHS Highland

" NHS Highland and both Highland and Argyll and Bute Council jointly fund independent advocacy; partly in response to our legislative responsibilities under the Mental Health Act*, but more importantly, in recognition of the need to support the most vulnerable people in our communities, by allowing them to have fair and equal access to services which enable them to have a stronger voice and more control over their lives. In order to avoid areas of potential conflict and ensure their loyalties lie only with the individual or group, this needs to be provided at arms length from other services.

Independent advocacy benefits local communities in a number of ways. For people who use advocacy services it provides a safeguard for vulnerable adults and children, and empowers people who may rely on other health services. For local communities it provides a base of trained and supported individuals who have an understanding of inequalities that exist and the needs of vulnerable people in their community. Therefore, it benefits communities overall by ensuring that systems and barriers are challenged to everyone's benefit and empowers individuals to take action for their own and their community's behalf.

* Mental Health (Care and Treatment) (Scotland) Act 2003

Service providers can learn from independent advocacy in a variety of ways. It can lead to better decisions being made about a person's treatment and the services they receive leading to better outcomes; it can provide valuable information and feedback as well as healthy challenges to those who commission and provide services; it can provide constructive challenges to service providers and help professionals to redesign and refine the system so that it works better for everyone and it helps us to keep our focus on people who are most at risk.

It would be useful if independent advocacy organisations had access not only to public funding monies through commissioning, but also could maintain their independence and explore other models of provision or other vulnerable groups of people, through access to other forms of funding streams such as the lottery or other grant awarding bodies. There is also a need to explore the impact of legislation i.e. the Mental Health Act*, on vulnerable groups and individuals not included in this. An example is people with Autistic Spectrum Disorders or people with physical disabilities as well as communities such as Black and Minority Ethnic and homeless people...

...Finally, I would like to see independent advocacy offered in a variety of ways that provides the best choices for individuals, such as individual professional advocacy; collective advocacy; citizen advocacy and support for self-advocacy. ,,

"It's brilliant, now I have friends and people to talk to."
Bobby Heron, Advocating Together Self Advocacy Group

Linda, Bobby and Kenny...

… are all members of the Advocating Together Self Advocacy Group. They meet once a week and discuss any issues that people have. They support each other to speak up for themselves.

" Sometimes we sit and have cups of tea and a chat. Other times the Local Authority or Health Board bring things that they want people with learning disabilities to understand such as posters and leaflets. We test it out and then go out to meet other folk with learning disabilities to see what they think about it. And then we tell the Local Authority or Health Board. "

"Before I was in advocacy, I didn't have a voice, now I speak to people, that's the best thing that ever happened."

death life success failure

and advocacy

> " Some years ago Rupert, in his late seventies, was admitted to a care home from another part of the country. Everybody, other than those who moved him, agreed he was wrongly placed – even the staff of the home. Rupert was told he was "suffering from a cognitive deficit" and needed to be cared for. However, he was quite lucid and clear about his dislike of the place in which he had, in his own words, 'been dumped'.
>
> I spent days and months and years negotiating with legal and welfare agencies to secure a better deal for him, but eventually had to admit defeat. Last month Rupert died. The last years of his life had given him a place to live with certain qualities of security, but at the same time he suffered badly from being lifted out of his home environment and parachuted into alien surroundings.

Maurice and Kenneth are two patients who have spent long years in psychiatric and custodial settings, for them these years have seen intensive advocacy on their behalf for appropriate community placements. At first it was argued they were not suitable candidates for this, but as other long-stay patients with no less severe problems were positively resettled, attitudes changed. Too late, however, as no planning for accommodation had been done for them and largely for this reason they were knocked back by their respective tribunals.

Ironically Maurice's tribunal, a spectacularly unpleasant affair, happened on the same day as Rupert's funeral. I would very much have liked to attend that, perhaps in search of some minimal degree of closure, but missed the train by ten minutes.

I feel a sense of failure at all this, not by way of a crippling guilt at my own inadequacy, but grounded in the huge odds against which we always seem to be pitted. This is to a large extent because those whom we are engaged to support are at the bottom of the heap, not just in terms of their mental disorder, but with the added vulnerability of physical ill-health which accompanies it...

...Maurice, Kenneth, and others in the same unit, have fragile existences circumscribed by a poverty-stricken institutional environment and impending death. A number of patients have passed away at a relatively early age before they were afforded the opportunity for a fuller life. They have been failed...

I have not recounted any advocacy 'successes', mainly because I usually avoid that word. I don't like the word 'failed' either but have used it here because that is what happens to people like Rupert, Maurice and Kenneth. They are not failures; they **are failed** by ubiquitous bumbling mediocrities. As independent advocacy workers, we share in the outworking of that process of failing people, and with the patients, have to bear some of the pain and the cost. We need a survival strategy for that, not for our own self-preservation, but so that the voices of those on the margins can go on being sounded until they are heard and listened to and given life.

,,

Advocacy is...

..."The freedom to do and say what is right, rather than being afraid."

Alison Murphy - Dunfermline Advocacy Initiative

Mary

" I have been involved in supporting carers for around 8-9 years. I first became involved in independent advocacy after I was originally a carer myself.

The ideal qualities of an advocate for carers are someone who would defend a carer and carers' needs. They would have the ability to be impersonal and detached. "

James

" In November 1999 I was diagnosed with dementia, I couldn't do things that I used to take for granted, like driving and counting money - even though I used to work in a bank! I was at very low ebb. I sat at home depressed. I didn't go out, didn't wash, change clothes and didn't shave. Brenda helped me get my life back on track. She helped me sort out lots of things in my life; filling in forms and helping me do things I never thought were possible...

...Advocates are angels, I do things now that I couldn't do before I was diagnosed with dementia!...

...Public speaking used to terrify me, my mouth would feel like it had been poured with concrete. Since November 1999 I've spoken at conferences around Scotland, in Ireland, Dominican Republic and even Beirut. At first, Brenda would come with me and stand right beside me for support, then, as my confidence grew Brenda stepped back a little further. Now I can deliver a speech and give presentations without any support at all.

Brenda also encouraged me to take up photography, she helped me fill in forms for funding for a calendar. She advocated to get me help to learn how to use a camera again. I now take a lot of photographs all around Scotland and have produced a book. I also took photos for this year's Alzheimer Scotland Christmas cards. Some of my photographs are in this book.

I am also a member of the of the Scottish Dementia Working Group, we have members all over Scotland and we go and give talks to people with dementia and are involved in responding to Government consultations on legislation that effects people with dementia and those that care for people with dementia. In 2002 we produced a help card for people with dementia. People with dementia can use the card to help them explain discreetly why they may need assistance in certain situations, like in shops and on buses. One of the symptoms of dementia is that you lose the ability to count money. This happened to me and I used to find it very embarrassing. A grown man who can't count his money in shops! That's why I wanted to produce the card, so that other people wouldn't need to feel like I did.

"

Photograph by James McKillop

"Until the great mass of the people shall be filled with the sense of responsibility for each others' welfare, social justice can never be attained."

Helen Keller

Glynis and Calum

Glynis is an advocate at Barnardo's Hear 4 U Children's Rights and Advocacy. She has had an advocacy partnership with Calum since October 2006, when he was referred to the Barnardo's project by a guidance teacher at his school.

Hear 4 U provide advocacy for any young person up to the age of 20 in South Ayrshire with issues affecting their mental health and emotional wellbeing.

Calum's story

" In autumn 2006, I was at a very low point of my life. I had a lot of problems in school as I'd missed a lot of coursework. There were prelims just over a month away and I was struggling to keep on top of the work. I also had a meeting with Guidance and Management about my attendance due in January.

Outside school, I was taking a lot of stress out on my parents and they both had problems of their own at the time and things were like a war zone at home. I was also having problems with anxiety and depression as a result of harassment within my school and outside. I was struggling to get the school to understand the situation. They didn't seem to be taking into consideration the reasons for my skiving, only that I was doing it...

...After Glynis got involved, things changed a lot.

...She was able to speak to my guidance teacher on my behalf, explain situations and reach big compromises with her about my school work. She also made sure that the guidance staff were made aware of my views and feelings on things within the school.

When the J.A.T meeting (the meeting with Management and Guidance) eventually happened, I was a lot more comfortable with it, having had help from Glynis. She helped me to prepare beforehand and having her with me in the meeting helped to make sure I got my points across and the school took them seriously.

As well as this, Glynis provided a lot of resources on handling stress and anxiety that have helped me a lot, even up to now with the final exams approaching fast! I'm a lot more confident in myself now, and less worried about losing control of things or getting out of my depth. "

Glynis's story

" When I first met Calum, he was anxious and depressed. When he told me how he felt, I encouraged him to make an appointment to talk to his doctor, who then referred him to the Child and Adolescent Mental Health Team for support.

I have found my partnership with Calum very rewarding and it has been great to see his resilience improve and although we are still in an advocacy partnership, Calum is becoming more confident in self advocating in most situations. He is now considering joining our advisory group and has agreed to take part in interviews for a new worker.

Calum clearly says that he now feels others are listening to him and taking his views into consideration before making decisions and judgements about him. He now feels more involved in this process. "

Alan

'Advocating to get the message across'

Steve (not his real name) has been treated for depression and schizophrenia and has harboured suicidal thoughts and feelings. He lives on his own in his council flat in Edinburgh where in the last few months he has been bullied, physically assaulted and threatened with a knife by known drug abusers. They have repeatedly robbed him of his money, they have broken into his flat and stolen his television and stereo. They have kicked in his door several times and created a disturbance at all times of the night to the point that Steve considers he has no option but to start living rough. Some weeks ago Steve vacated his flat as he feels safer living on the streets during the day, sleeping in a cemetery at night. Going to the police, for him, he says, is not an option.

Julie (again not her real name) is a 30 year old single mother of two children under the age of 5. She lives on the 11th floor of an ageing block of council flats. She too suffers from depression and from time to time has expressed suicidal feelings. The area round about and the damp and dingy stairwell are littered with cans, bits of broken glass, condoms and needles. There are often patches of dried blood. Not unnaturally, Julie fears for herself and her children. Julie has applied to the Council to be re-housed but competition is fierce with over 4000 expressions of interest every fortnight. Her chances will be significantly improved were she to be awarded health priority and although she has the backing of her Consultant, GP, Health Visitor and Support Worker, her representations are re-buffed by the Council without explanation or word of a right of appeal which she is entitled to in terms of the Council Letting Policy. She even enlisted the support of her MP but no one, it seems, is listening. Julie's health is beginning to deteriorate.

This is real life Edinburgh, the Festival City, 2006. Steve and Julie are among an increasing number of mental health service users who are taking advantage of the services of trained volunteer advocacy workers to help get their message across and be heard. One of the reasons behind the increase is that while the concept of patient advocacy has been long established, particularly in a hospital and social services environment, advocacy is accorded statutory recognition for the first time in the Mental Health (Care and Treatment) (Scotland) Act 2003 the main provisions of which came into force in October. Responsibility is placed firmly on the Local Authority acting in tandem with the Health Board to secure the availability of advocacy services for persons with a mental disorder and to see that those services are made use of. "Mental disorder" encompasses not just mental illness but personality disorder and learning disability...

...Advocacy is not about giving advice but rather assisting individuals to express their own views and preferences...

...In practice, what this amounts to is help with the often stress-inducing trials and tribulations of day to day living. The advocacy worker is there to side with the service user, to listen, to encourage, to explore options and to communicate. There may be a problem with housing or benefits entitlement; often there are issues over care and treatment including medication which have to be talked through with a Consultant or GP; perhaps there is a dispute with neighbours or it might just be that assistance is required with the form filling which has become such a mesmerising grind of daily life. There are few of us, after all, who have not experienced stultifying mind numbing encounters with layer upon layer of officialdom in one guise or another. And just being there for the service user can be a great leveller, enough to make "the other side" sit up and take notice, the difference between being listened to and being fobbed off or ignored.

AdvoCard is one independent charity providing advocacy services which has just celebrated its 10th anniversary. The services, covering the whole of Edinburgh are delivered in the main through trained volunteer advocacy workers although a smaller specialist team has been developed to concentrate on issues relating to those who are subject to compulsory treatment under the Act.

AdvoCard has a bank of around 40 active volunteers from a wide cross section of the community. Most volunteers work on short term engagements. Others will work with individual service users on a longer term basis, perhaps up to a year at a time. Training is constantly updated and in anticipation of increased take-up of services, recruitment programmes are being run on a continual basis.

Whether Councils and Health Boards are doing enough to promote advocacy, only time will tell. The 2003 Act* is undoubtedly one of the Executive's legislative success stories and although the focus has been on a bespoke Mental Health Tribunal system which replaces the role of the Sheriff Courts, and the new procedures for dealing with the compulsory treatment of patients in hospital and the community, the part played by the unsung volunteer advocacy worker in underpinning care in the community should not be underestimated...

...One thing is for sure – advocacy is a valuable safeguard to have in the struggle to reinforce rights and respect for those with a mental disorder...

* Mental Health (Care and Treatment) (Scotland) 2003

...Edinburgh may well be the fourth largest financial centre in Europe and a major player in the world of wealth creativity but just down the road, there is a sadder, sombre, darker side to life...

...And what of Steve and Julie? Both Steve and Julie consulted AdvoCard. Although Steve is a Council tenant he was technically homeless and entitled at the very least to temporary alternative accommodation from the Council. Several phone calls from a volunteer advocate led to a series of meetings with the Council's Housing Options Scheme which secured temporary bed and breakfast accommodation for Steve in another part of the city. Julie seemed to be banging her head against a bureaucratic brick wall when she consulted AdvoCard. The obfuscation and procrastination has continued but she is not giving up. AdvoCard continues to help her fight her corner and her voice is getting louder and clearer.

Margaret and Anne

Margaret has two daughters, both of whom have additional support needs. Originally, like most people, she found it hard to challenge authority and she didn't realise that you needed to. It can be difficult to question professionals, especially when you believe that they know best. Speaking up for people was not something Margaret found particularly natural, however, through interaction with the agencies and professionals who dealt with her daughters, she learnt to...

...When she read about citizen advocacy she thought "I've been doing that!"...

...She has been a citizen advocate for Anne for 18 months, although she had previously met her partner in a professional capacity and had known about her for a number of years. Anne has a learning difficulty with limited and repetitive speech and an unexplained psychosis.

Anne has no family and although she never had nursing home needs, she was placed in a nursing home around 15 years ago. Margaret kept reminding care workers that she was inappropriately placed. On several occasions when Margaret referred Anne to get a place in supported accommodation she was turned down. After a little investigation, Margaret discovered that the Care Home Manager had described Anne as aggressive and feared that she may attack people if she lived in a house. Margaret fought to get this opinion changed, Anne wasn't aggressive, she simply didn't like the noise and clamour of a nursing home, home to 50 people. Because she was unable to effectively communicate this, she tried to push noisy people away. Anne now lives in a house with 4 other women. The move has changed Anne completely.

The most noticeable improvement in Margaret's eyes, was when she introduced Anne to her husband. Anne has a standard spiel that she regurgitates when she meets new people and Margaret had forgotten she did this until it happened in front of her husband. Margaret realised that Anne didn't do this with her anymore, meaning that she must be completely comfortable in her company.

Part of Margaret's role has been to put Anne in touch with the services that she needs. Margaret felt that Anne had a lot of potential communication that was inhibited and so put her in touch with a speech and language therapist and an art therapist, activities she now really enjoys.

Margaret recognises that Anne may not have seen and done many things that other people take for granted, and so she lets her have as many new experiences as possible. In particular she enjoys going for trips in Margaret's car, going for coffee at her house and going for walks.

Anne has met her husband and her daughters and Margaret has given her photos of each of her family members so that she remembers who they are. She has also given her a group photo with her in it so that she feels she is a part of their family life.

Advocacy is...

..."about addressing the imbalance of power."

"First they ignore you, then they laugh at you, then they fight you, then you win."

Mohandas Gandhi

No Bullying Allowed Team

'No bullying allowed!'

FBS provide advocacy for young people with disabilities or additional support needs, and for carers with educational issues arising from the ASL* Act.

They ran a self advocacy group which raised concerns about bullying both within school and their local community. The children told them stories about not being listened to by teachers, adults and even the local police. With the aid of their advocate, Kathryn, the group wanted to do something that would help people listen to their concerns and take their issues seriously.

*Education (Additional Support for Learning) (Scotland) Act 2004

Kathryn

" As a group we applied to Comic Relief to fund the production of a cartoon style DVD that we would use to tell other young people and teachers about the seriousness of bullying.

The group took part in a number of activities including drama and photo story telling to help them express their concerns and share them with student animators who we had contracted from Motherwell College. Our group worked with a second group of young people in a different area of our Local Authority who also wanted to give their input to the project as they too had concerns about bullies and bullying. They met weekly and worked together to share ideas with the animators and collate a series of activities to be included in a workbook that would accompany the DVD.

On completion of the project we held a launch and a number of the young people wrote presentations or speeches to present to the audience. This was attended by almost 100 people including a local MSP, representatives from the Education Authority, Social Work Department, ChildLine, Scottish Youth Parliament, school pupil councils and other local organisations...

...It was a real success!

After the launch we were invited to a couple of local schools to present our work and they took the pack that we had produced to use in their schools. Then the Education Authority invited us to a meeting for local guidance teachers from schools across North Lanarkshire to present our work. They supported the use of our DVD and workbook in schools.

The children and young people presented their work again and additional teenagers who had contacted our one – to – one advocacy service regarding bullying also spoke to teachers about their experiences.

This all helped in increasing awareness of the seriousness of bullying in schools and communities and gave the young people involved greater confidence in themselves and their abilities. Some of the children have written about what it meant to be involved in the project...

...This is ongoing work and the next step is to target other local authorities to get their schools using our work 'No Bullying Allowed'.

The Commissioner's Perspective

Dr. Mary Harper, Planning and Commissioning Manager for NHS Dumfries and Galloway

NHS Dumfries and Galloway, in partnership with Dumfries and Galloway Council, has funded 'generic' advocacy services for many years as we believe that it is important that people can give their views on the health and social care they receive. It is often the most vulnerable people in society who have most difficulty in being heard, and we have an obligation to help them express their wishes. We now also have a statutory duty, through the Mental Health Act*, to make independent advocacy available to people with a mental disorder...

...Independent advocacy allows the views of vulnerable people and people at vulnerable times to be heard and acknowledged...

...This should hopefully reduce some of the health inequalities that are unfortunately prevalent. There has been a welcome shift in health and social care from doing things 'to' people, to doing things 'with' people across the statutory, voluntary and private sectors. These sectors seem increasingly keen to work with independent advocacy services to help their clients. As we know that the more control people feel they have over their life, the greater their feeling of wellbeing; this should have a positive impact across the community.

*Mental Health (Care and Treatment) (Scotland) Act 200:

Advocacy has enabled treatment plans to be enhanced, with the views of patients/clients being taken into account. There is more confidence in a care package/pathway even when all the patient's preferences have not been met. There is evidence that when people are more involved in their treatment plans there is a greater chance of success. This in turn means the treatment is more likely to work, and so improve health.

As part of the local NHS complaints procedure we've been able to offer referral to advocacy for people who need and want it. In such cases most complaints are addressed through resolution, with clients feeling listened to...

...I would welcome more citizen advocacy for people who have a recurring need for advocacy, such as people with a learning disability.

Also, in the future, I see there being an increasing need for advocates specialising in dementia as we expect an increase in people with Alzheimer's in Dumfries and Galloway, due to our ageing population.

Advocacy

by Deborah Nidorro

Deborah first found out about advocacy through her brother in law. She got involved because she wanted to develop a support network, a body to minute school meetings. Her advocate has helped her with many issues, too many to mention! Deborah has found that having an advocate has made an immense difference to her life and describes it as the difference between standing alone and enabling oneself to move on.

Many people in life lack confidence to speak
What they need to voice.
I just want them to know they have another choice.
In this day and age no one should suffer alone
especially with issues on their mind.
I want them to know there is an organisation called
Independent Advocacy they can access and find.

As for me I am very assertive but can have problems
trying to express.
Having Attention – Deficit – Hyperactivity – Disorder
can make my mind work so fast.
 "Sorry I've forgotten that question I'm still trying to
comprehend the last."

I cannot talk and write and concentrate and focus at the same time.
This would make my head feel like it was going to explode.
Then I would simply need to go.

I sense sitting very close to me my advocate by my side.
Not only is this service 100% free but honestly means so much to me.

I am always treated with empathy.
I am always treated with respect.

I have informed the advocate worker where my deficits lay.
Then we plan our agenda if we have a meeting on the way.

I honestly never knew such a helpful organisation existed in my own home town.
I thought there must be a misunderstanding receiving such immense support for free.
It was my brother in law who gave the number to me.

Shona, Sandra, Norrie

I mean this straight from my big soft heart.
I thank each and every one of you for the assistance you provide.

There are many people out there who cannot cope, so hide.

Keith

The Murray Foundation

The Murray Foundation is a support group based in Scotland which provides various levels of support to people who have suffered limb loss. It was clearly evident from visits to patients both at home and in hospitals, that they had other types of problems that needed to be solved, many of a financial nature. It was decided that a pilot advocacy service be set up and I took on the role of the advocate.

" In April 2007 I visited Tom in central Scotland. He'd been in a road accident many years ago and had his leg amputated due to pain and infection. He was recovering well, however one task he could not face was completing a Disability Living Allowance application form, or should I say application book! In my personal opinion completing one of these forms can look overwhelming, especially when you are not in the best frame of mind after surgery and are coming to terms with major changes in your life.

TOM

...Anyway, I sat down with Tom and between us we completed the form with me doing the scribing...

...It wasn't too long before Tom received a letter advising him that he had been successful with his application and his initial payment that was backdated to the date that his form had been submitted was for a tidy four figure sum.

However Tom's biggest problem was his gas bills, which were usually £50 per month. When in hospital recovering from his operation, his sister brought up his mail one day and Tom opened up one from the gas supplier which contained his most recent bill and found it to be nearly £900! In his heart he knew it could not be right, but how could he sort it out, especially as he was in hospital?

His sister tried hard, however she lost patience with the 'press 1 to speak to an advisor' then wait twenty minutes in a queue until getting cut off!

So I took over and had what can only be described as a battle with the gas supplier. While going through the process of having previous bills checked, meter readings taken and having discussions with the gas supplier, Tom continued to receive letters threatening legal action, supply cut off and Sheriff Officers coming to his house. The wording of these letters can be very frightening and intimidating and even though the gas supplier advised me nothing would happen, their computers kept churning out these letters.

The gas supplier was adamant they were correct. However, during one of many phone call discussions I was advising them of a meter reading I had taken and suddenly the penny dropped at the other end of the line. The meter being used was "imperial" however it was being read by the gas supplier as metric! Sincere apologies followed and by now the amount outstanding was approximately £1,600.

The account was adjusted to what was the correct figure (about £600), meantime, Tom had been putting money aside on a monthly basis so he was able to pay what he owed...

...He even received a cheque for £100 from the gas supplier as an apology for the stress and upset they had caused and I was glad to see him smiling again.

Robert from Glasgow was a different type of case altogether. Robert had lost his leg due to diabetes but was unable to use an artificial limb. In all other ways he had fully recovered but he was desperate to go home to where he had lived most of his life...   ROBERT

...Before I became involved Robert had spent 12 months occupying a NHS bed whilst debates raged on about adapting his council house or finding him alternative accommodation...

...Robert had been a builder and believed changes could be made to the structure of the house so his wheelchair and other equipment could be moved in and out of his house. The local council thought otherwise and their arguments did not satisfy Robert. There had been a string of meetings with a lot of people involved that Robert found extremely frustrating. In some cases meetings came to a halt as Robert lost his temper, shouting and swearing at everybody, and on one occasion throwing chairs around the room. Robert was going home and he was not going to give up and be sent to a nursing home!

By the time I met Robert everybody had put the fear of death into me and I had been given the impression he was unreasonable, pig headed and violent! When we first met, it was the exact opposite. Robert was very honest with me and a key point was that he said:...

" Look, I can't talk like these people and can't put over what I want to say very well. I need someone to help me and keep me from losing my temper."

...I replied that I would help him and in all the meetings Robert always remained calm and reasonable, trusting me to deal with his case...

...I took a different approach. I asked the social services if they had been to the house to see if the work could be done, but their reply was that they didn't need to as they had "reports"...

...I pushed and pushed the point of "let's all go to the house and if we all agree the work cannot be done, fine. Otherwise if we agree it can, we should as a group, make it happen"...

...I had only been in the house five minutes, along with several people from the council and social services, when it became clear to me the work could be done and the council officials were embarrassed enough to agree. So much for the reports, you can't beat seeing things for yourself before making a judgement...

...Within a couple of months the work was completed, Robert went home and the NHS could admit another patient. Myself? This case gave me the most satisfaction of all.

99

Alan

Alan is one of a number of volunteers who work on a one to one basis for an advocacy organisation called AdvoCard, which specialises in helping people with mental health problems.

Alan first developed an interest in advocacy after responding to an advertisement by AdvoCard in the Scotsman newspaper. He has now been a volunteer advocacy worker for three years.

" As a solicitor I have worked in the field of medical law for many years, looking after the interests of the Health Boards and the wider NHS, but seeing things from the other side has been an eye opener. On occasion it can seem akin to David against Goliath, which only serves to emphasise just how important the role of the advocate is.

" My strong sense of fair play means there is never any lack of motivation, but what can be difficult and frustrating, particularly where I see that the service user is not being accorded the respect he or she deserves, is having to stop short of giving advice. The advocate is not there to advise, but rather to listen, support, explore options and provide a voice.

I have helped my advocacy partners resolve a variety of problems or disputes concerning homelessness, housing, repairs, benefits entitlement and other tussles with officialdom. My experience has shown me that sometimes simply being there can be enough to make a difference.

Measuring just how successful a piece of advocacy work has been is not always easy. In many cases, once the job is complete, the service user departs from the scene and does not return. One troubled lady who did return two weeks after an initial meeting, spoke of having left AdvoCard offices "walking on air" and having felt as if she had been on holiday in the intervening period. Sharing the burden and providing support and a voice had given her a significant lift and the confidence to take control of her problems. "

Being an advocate is...

..."focusing on the needs of the client and helping people to make a difference to their own lives."

Bonnie Holligan - Positive Voice

Linda

Linda is a peer advocate for Dundee Independent Advocacy Support (DIAS). DIAS provides advocacy for people with learning difficulties, dementia, physical disabilities and frail older people.

"The peer advocates at DIAS are all people with disabilities."

Linda Sheridan - peer advocate,
Dundee Independent Advocacy Support

" I was first introduced to peer advocacy by the peer volunteer co-ordinator. She introduced me to the rest of the group and I decided it would be a good thing to do. We had four weeks of training. There were lots of activities and I loved it. I thought, "This is for me!" I was not sure that I had passed but was told I had passed with flying colours.

We went up to the hospital and I met my advocacy partner. She has been in hospital for years; I don't think that's fair. She is probably getting a house with 24/7 support in the community and I hope it is suitable for her.

I visit her once a fortnight. Mostly we sit and draw as she has no speech. When I visit she is all over me. I think she really enjoys my visits. I don't know what other visitors she has. I will still visit her in her own house when she moves. I'm not going to lose contact now that I have struck up a relationship with her.

The peer advocates at DIAS are all people with disabilities. Some people think if you have a learning disability you are stupid. They don't realise what we are capable of doing. I also help in a charity shop and have a paid job with another organisation. For DIAS I go to national conferences, help with recruitment and am now an assistant trainer for new peer advocates.

I absolutely adore what I do! "

'the Midas touch'

" In independent advocacy there is an important distinction between allowing people to have their aspirations and raising their expectations unduly about what can be achieved.

I thought I had that one sorted in my mind until I met Jessie. Somehow the bit about expectations was to spiral out of control. Her confidence in my ability to make things happen terrified me.

Jessie, a lady with severe Parkinson's disease, was struggling to cope with daily living in her council house. When she made me a cup of tea she shook so much I wondered which of us would end up wearing the hot drink! When she tried to go out, she would get 'stuck' on the road and be unable to step up on to the kerb.

Jessie talked a bit about money. She had applied twice, with support from a professional, for Attendance Allowance. I could not understand why she had been turned down, as she seemed to fit the criteria very easily. I knew it was not my job, but she agreed to allow me to help with the form and to re-apply once more. She had been reluctant to agree but when this application was successful, she was delighted, and so was I.

From then on I had the Midas touch!...

...I could do no wrong and she had a seemingly unshakeable faith in my ability to achieve whatever she wished. Initially, I was flattered. Visiting her was a definite ego boost but I soon began to feel uncomfortable. I'd never be able to keep it up.

Jessie told me how she felt she needed more support and we discussed options. Her favoured one was to move into very sheltered housing; she had heard that meals would be provided but she would still have her own flat. I agreed to find out what I could about what was available and go back to see her.

When I went back, she had already done some research herself and told me exactly which very sheltered housing complex she had chosen. I tried to explain that it would take some time, especially since that particular complex only had 10 flats and there would be a waiting list. Perhaps she would like to look at widening her choice? She was adamant. She knew what she wanted and thought I would be able to get it for her.

Back at the office, I phoned the council to ask how many very sheltered houses were let each year. The answer did not inspire confidence. On my next visit to Jessie I was determined to prepare her for possible disappointment, or at least for a long time on a waiting list, but she hardly listened. She was more interested in telling me about having donated her dining table to charity and asking me if I knew anyone who would like her fridge freezer. She reckoned it would be too large for the new flat. Which new flat? This was not how independent advocacy was meant to turn out. Help!

Next time I visited I tried again, explaining about waiting lists and how very few houses were available. To no avail! I had a great deal of difficulty in getting away without accepting two table lamps, a vase and a telephone table!...

...It was depressing to imagine visiting regularly over the next year or so and seeing her house gradually empty of furniture at the same time as her faith in me evaporated...

...All turned out really well, however. To my surprise and delight but just as Jessie expected, she was offered a flat in the complex of her choice and moved in within a matter of months. I'll never understand how I developed the Midas touch with Jessie. It certainly has not been evident in my life before or since. But I am now very wary of people who think advocates have a magic wand!

Being an advocate is...

..."a job that counts which I continue to enjoy. I can't think of any job I'd rather do."

Linda Coates - Advocacy Matters, Greater Glasgow

Steve

"

I heard about advocacy by word of mouth from people that I knew who were already members of the local People First Group. This was first in 1994 in Fraserburgh then a year later I got involved in People First in Edinburgh.

I got involved with People First because I felt that the group had an understanding of the problems I face...

...People First is different from most other self-advocacy organisations because we, the people who are members, run it...

...We have between 70 and 80 local groups, covering the whole of Scotland. Most of the groups are based in local communities. Some are based in long-stay hospitals.

All the members of the local groups in an area elect members from their area to represent them on the National Board of Directors. The Board manages the staff, who are there in a support and advisory role. But it is the members who have the final say. I have been a Board member for 12 years and in April 2007 I was elected as Vice Chair of People First (Scotland).

...There are so many issues we are involved in. They include health, transport, housing and benefits...

...In the groups we meet as members and discuss our concerns about any of the above issues or any other issue which a member wants to discuss that may be affecting them personally.

Members of People First can get as involved as they like. Some people just like to come along to the groups to meet people and hear what is happening. Some people like to raise issues at their local groups. Other people like to be more involved in putting forward the views of people with learning difficulties by attending meetings with professionals and government ministers.

A recent example of our work has been about members getting bus passes. A lot of our members, me included, were having difficulty getting forms signed to get concessionary bus passes because the information was not accessible. It did not clearly say who could sign the form. So another member and I wrote a letter to Transport Scotland to highlight our concerns. Because I also represent People First at the Same As You Implementation Group, I was also able to express our concerns to the Transport Scotland representative in person at one of the meetings...

The outcome of this is that some People First staff are now able to sign the bus pass forms and our members have been made more aware of how the application system works. This is because the information that we find out at a national level can be shared by the Directors when they return to their own areas and local groups...

...You see advocacy is not just about speaking out, but also about building the skills and confidence to do this in a way that people will listen to and respect what we are saying...

...I would definitely encourage anybody with learning difficulties to get involved with a People First group because People First feels like a family to me. There is a close bond between members and staff which you do not get with every organisation. The big difference for me is the members are the ones with the power. It lets them feel involved and in control.

,,

Photograph by James McKillop

Ashley and Louise

Ashley is 21 and has been a citizen advocate for Louise for the last 3 years. Louise is 22 and has severe epilepsy, to the extent that it has caused her brain damage and she has a seizure about once a day. She spends most of her life in a wheelchair and is only allowed to walk on flat surfaces indoors, when she wears a helmet. Louise lives in residential care for young people but is now facing a move to a home for adults. Ashley is the only friend who visits Louise and their relationship is very important to both of them.

When Ashley was Student President at her college, the local citizen advocacy organisation gave a talk to try to attract people for their young persons' project. Ashley and Louise were matched because Ashley is very artistic, and her co-ordinator thought that it would be good for Louise to have someone who could communicate with her in a creative way, since she has no verbal communication bar a few sounds.

When Ashley speaks to Louise she exaggerates everything she says so that the conversation appears more interesting. Louise may not understand what Ashley is saying but she will understand the highs and lows in her voice. Ashley also entertains Louise by giving her something to play with, even if it is just a bangle. They often see each other after Ashley finishes work.

Ashley views her partnership with Louise just like any other friendship. She visits her as regularly as she would visit any of her other friends. She has also been trained in how to administer Louise's medication in case she takes a seizure while they're out together. This gives Ashley the freedom to take Louise for outings alone. Together they go to the cinema and out for dinner with Ashley's friends. Ashley strongly believes that if people don't accept Louise, they don't accept her and she doesn't want to be their friend.

Together they raised money for breast cancer research by taking part in the Race for Life, where Ashley pushed Louise all the way, and although they came last, they raised £150 and Louise had the chance to raise money to help other people...

...Ashley is the only person who visits Louise through choice and who isn't family or a professional...

...In the world of professionals, Louise has no voice, this has led to Ashley speaking up on her behalf. Ashley wouldn't expect to be treated like that, so why should others treat Louise like that? Ashley found out that a nurse at the home was limiting everyone to 3 nappies a day. To Ashley this didn't make sense, of course people go to the toilet more than 3 times a day! So why should this not be the case for people without a voice? By speaking with her co-ordinator at the citizen advocacy organisation and writing letters to people in authority, she managed to get the situation changed.

Her friendship with Louise has also widened her eyes to the capabilities of someone with learning difficulties. During the day, Ashley works in a fast food restaurant and her experience with Louise has taught her that people with learning difficulties can make their own decisions and have their own mind. She applies what she's learnt to her day to day life and has also advised her colleagues about how to communicate with customers with learning difficulties.

Diff'rently The

Just look through my eyes
And then surely you'll see
The spirit of the person
Still deep down within me
But when I'm looking outwards
I' still me despite being, so much
Diff'rently The Same

Mmm-Mmm things easy before
Can be much harder now
A-a fond memory sought
Will furrow my brow
Amidst all of this turmoil
Doggedness enables me, to cope
Diff'rently The Same

I am still your friend, from your far off schooldays
Your ever – loving spouse ever since our wedding day
I'm still your father, your mother who
Was forever there when you were needing me most
I'm your big sister, your little brother
I' the person who needs all of your understanding
Though things inside me are changing
I still love you all though I've become
So Diff'rently The Same

Same

By James McKillop

Odd looks come my way
When I fail to disguise
A feeling lost expression
That comes clouding my eyes
But what's the alternative
To sitting housebound feeling, sadly
Diff'rently The Same

Mmm-Mmm friends of bygone years
Don't know how to react
Some speak past me in hushed tones
Others have less tact
And fidget in my presence
Yet some day they might also, become
Diff'rently The Same

Cath and Irene

Cath and Irene have been in an advocacy partnership for 10 years. During this time Cath has helped Irene with many situations that have affected her life and enabled her to become the strong, outgoing person that she is today, with the ability to self advocate. Over time they have battled together on issues surrounding benefits and housing, medication, treatment and legal matters...

…Cath has accompanied Irene to meetings when she has felt less able to speak for herself. Advocating for her, Cath has made sure that Irene's thoughts are heard...

…Although Irene is a highly capable, confident person, with the ability to manage many day to day aspects of her life, she has struggled with an ongoing battle with depression. This is a problem that has stemmed from a troubled relationship with her mother and consequently affected her relationships with other family members. This has been of great anguish to her as it's often made it very difficult for her to form bonds with her family, and despite the friendship she has with some relations, she feels that she is

On many occasions, Cath has acted as a lifeline for Irene, as a voice to trust amongst a crowd who she feels wants to pull her down. She says often by simply talking and sharing the problem with Cath it seems more manageable. She has a way of turning an issue or a situation that seems colossal and overwhelming into something that is manageable and can be tackled. Irene says that Cath helped save her life.

Throughout their long relationship, Cath has often been one of the only people who knows Irene's full life story. Cath has experienced the full swing of Irene's emotions, so there is a mutual understanding and trust between the two of them. Cath attended Irene's 60th birthday party, which was a very special day for her...

...Irene sees advocacy as something that is a part of her life. It has given her a relationship with someone who she can trust, who will listen to her when she needs.

...Irene is now in the process of writing about her life, in part as a therapeutic exercise, but also to create a greater awareness of how troubled family relationships can impinge on your happiness in later life.

Advocacy is...

..."Being able to provide a valuable voice for those who are unable to express themselves."

Rik Hodgson - Positive Voice

An advocate...

...“Is someone who is on the side of the oppressed.”

Alison Murphy - Dunfermline Advocacy Initiative

The Mental Health Tribunal for Scotland and the role of the advocate

By Joyce Mouriki

As a general member of the Mental Health Tribunal for Scotland, I would like to give you my personal views of advocacy within the tribunal setting. I have long admired the work of independent advocates.

" I am a service user myself and sit on the Boards of two user involvement organisations. I have, in those capacities, been working alongside advocacy organisations both locally in Lanarkshire and nationally on varied pieces of work from local mental health service implementation to the wider national mental health agenda.

I would like however, to concentrate on the advocate's role within the tribunals that I have taken part in. The role seemed to vary depending on the individual service user, however unstintingly the advocate offers support. Usually they are a comforting physical presence, choosing to sit next to the service user. Very often they are the person turned to repeatedly by the service user to help them to clarify issues presented on the day.

The service user's legal representative will usually have presented the case and the advocate will help sometimes by reading a prepared statement on behalf of the service user. Sometimes they will just support the service user to make their own statement and sometimes they will make a statement on their behalf, having conferred throughout.

Occasionally the advocate will go to the tribunal alone when the service user chooses not to appear and in those circumstances the advocate reads a pre prepared statement at the service user's behest.

The advocates are enormously helpful to all, especially the service user and their families. In my opinion they help to make the tribunals a place where service user participation is maximised and they help to turn the principles of the Act* into practise. **,,**

* Mental Health (Care and Treatment) (Scotland) Act 2003

"A small group of thoughtful people could change the world. Indeed it's the only thing that ever has."

Margaret Mead

Sam

Sam attends a Day Centre and is a popular, cheerful man who has his own flat and appreciates all the help and support he gets...

...When the advocacy referral came through at first, the main contact was to be his brother who was his appointee and main carer. However, other family members contacted the recently appointed care manager and the advocate, making claims of neglect and exploitation.

Clearly there was a family feud going on and Sam was caught in the middle.

Sam spoke openly to his advocate but said he didn't want his brother, to get into trouble or to fall out with him –"It'll be okay" was his regular phrase. Social Work Department investigations proved that Sam was being exploited. For example, he often went out in his friend's car and contributed to petrol costs, yet he had his own mobility vehicle. But no one had told him this, he believed the car belonged to his brother.

A series of home visits and reviews flagged up areas of concern and Sam was supported by his advocate to contribute to the action plan. With the action plan, Sam felt that he could cope with taking control of his life again as he had the appropriate support and safety measures in place.

This was a two year process which was extremely conflict ridden at times. During some meetings Sam and his advocate had to leave because he was so upset and quite frightened when voices were raised or accusations were made. When this happened, transcripts of the meetings were requested and were discussed later when Sam could handle things better, and his advocate would support him to respond as he wished...

....In summer 2007 Sam had his first short break for years, supported by a younger family member whose company Sam really enjoys...

...He is also better off on a monthly basis now that the money formerly used for his mobility vehicle is paid directly to him. Via the Independent Living Fund he now has a new home support and social support team that work with him on a one to one basis.

Regular advocacy input continues for reviews and person centred planning updates, and Sam is now thinking forward to what he'll do when he 'retires' from the Day Centre in 2010.

"We have created a society that does not allow opportunities for people to take care of themselves because we have denied them opportunities."

Mohammad Yunus

5 minutes

Jo McFarlane

5 minutes to go Jo…
Time to wind up now.
Next week we'll continue…but
For now take a hankie and dry your eyes.
The door is there.
You really must leave now. I know
It's hard.
Oh dear. I have another appointment
In 5 minutes.
Come now, there there…

Freddie

" I first heard about Dundee Independent Advocacy Support (DIAS) 6 or 7 years ago. I wanted to move from the residential home into my own place. My care manager, Tom, offered me some places to stay, but I didn't think I would like any of them.

I met my advocate, Mandy, in January 2005. She helped me at review meetings and supported me with my dream of moving out. I am now due to move to my new flat and I am looking forward to this, but am a bit nervous too.

In 2006, Damian asked if I wanted to get involved with the DIAS Peer Advocacy Project. I was interested so went on a training course to learn how I could help other people with learning disabilities. I have been supporting a man from Bridgefoot House who is now in his own flat. I visit him there and have a chat. Peer Advocacy has helped my own confidence and helped me speak up.

My best times at DIAS have been going to the DIAS 10 Year Civic Reception at the City Chambers in March 2006 and being on a stall publicising DIAS at the Dundee Flower Show in September 2006. I also enjoy the parties in the Queens' Hotel and any other social events.

I think DIAS is a great organisation. They help people and I enjoy being involved with them. "

"Our lives begin to end the day we become silent about things that matter."

Martin Luther King Jr.

"Be the change that you want to see in the world."

Mohandas Gandhi

Michael and Gill

MICHAEL " After finishing my degree in law and Masters in Human Rights, I was looking for some voluntary work, anything to do with human rights, and I came across advocacy. I now realise that the protection of people's human rights is at the very heart of advocacy. Advocacy is human rights work in its most fundamental form.

I first met Gill two years ago and have since worked with her on a number of specific issues including accessing medical records and sorting out college courses. I meet Gill once every two weeks in the same café but it's not a social occasion and we don't know one another's friends. This means that when we meet, Gill knows that it is her time and she can talk about what she wants, unlike a mutual friendship where she would also spend time listening to me talk about my life and my problems!...

...Over the time that we've been working together, I've seen Gill's confidence grow. She looks healthy and a glow has developed around her...

Gill now manages to sort lots of things out by herself. For example, she recently moved house and I had no idea. However, I don't see that there will be a time when our partnership will end...

...I have a normal relationship with her as there may always be something that creeps into her life that she needs my assistance with. I'm always learning new things about Gill and her life and this is what keeps it fresh and interesting.

GILL

My problems started when I was working as an auxiliary nurse and my manager bullied me so much that I was forced to leave. Once I left, I thought these problems wouldn't happen again but they did. I was going to college and again the bullying started. This was when it seriously began to affect my mental heath. I couldn't believe it was happening again. Health professionals and officials at my college told me that I was schizophrenic, when I knew that I wasn't. I was depressed. The whole situation had made me very ill...

...Having an advocate has helped me to gain the confidence to pursue my further education...

...I have been taking classes in maths. Next I hope to conquer the other sciences so that eventually I can go on to do forensic science. Initially Michael helped me by putting me in touch with the right people who could help with various matters. He helped me get access to my medical records so that I can see what has been written about me. My education is also very important to me and he has helped me sort out issues with the college. Being diagnosed as dyslexic at an early age, I feel that this is something that I have missed out on. ”

Billy

Billy goes to the Advocafé Group which was set up to provide a drop-in informal atmosphere for people to access advocacy. Group members gain experience of having conversations about things they may not have thought about before and are encouraged to share their opinions and feelings about things. When common issues arise, group members may choose to take action and are supported to make their feelings known. For example, the local Dial a Bus service stops at 6.30 at night which meant participants could use the bus to go out in the evenings but not to get home. Group members invited the scheme organisers to come and meet them to discuss this. Some people who come along have not experienced taking part in groups before.

" My name is Billy and since I've joined the advocacy it's helped me in a big way. When I first came to the advocacy organisation it was a group of people talking about all kinds of suggestions, like how they felt about themselves. I've talked about different issues and helped come up with ideas and other people have done the same. I enjoyed advocacy as I've met so many new friends from all walks of life and everyone is so nice and friendly, including the staff...

"A lot of bad things happen to people, not because workers are bad but because they are busy."

John O'Brien

Loraine

Partners in Advocacy provides advocacy to adults who use learning disability services, and children and young people with any additional support needs.

Loraine is a co-ordinator with Partners in Advocacy in Edinburgh.

" I worked for over 25 years with children and young people with learning disabilities, challenging behaviour and complex needs. After completing my SVQ and HNC I finally realised that I needed a new challenge.

My job is a result of a new post being created within Partners in Advocacy to advocate for children and young people in Edinburgh who had additional support needs.

This covers a huge range of young people not just those who have learning disabilities. We provide the opportunity for any child or young person to have an advocate to help support them with any issue they may have that impacts on their quality of life.

Advocating for someone who is non verbal is always a challenge but a very rewarding one. It may take longer to get to know them well, as you need to rely on different skills to be sure you have gathered all the relevant information to be able to advocate on their behalf.

I have worked with a young person with autism and challenging behaviour. He needed extra support to be able to remain at home. The package of care in place was not enough. I contacted the social work department for the allocation of a Social Worker and visited other service providers on behalf of the young person to see if they could support him. He has been able to remain at home with extra support put in place.

Another young person I worked with had Asperger's Syndrome and low self-esteem with high expectations from his family. He discussed with me some complex issues which he felt he could not share with others. I was able to refer him onto the relevant organisations, which were able to support him through these issues.

For successful results in advocacy you need time, patience and to think out of the box now and again. This helps your partner gain in confidence and helps support them on their journey to one day advocating for themselves. I get great satisfaction from each one of the young people I work with, through supporting their voice to be heard and to speak up.

Helen

Helen is a full time advocate with Advocacy Matters, Greater Glasgow. She has been working in professional advocacy for adults with mental health problems, aged 16 and over, for the last 20 months.

" I have a background as a specialist money advisor, and after moving to Glasgow in 2004 had been doing telephone advice work. I first became involved in advocacy in late 2005 when I saw a post with Advocacy Matters, and was interested in moving into advocacy.

Being an advocate allows me to work on a one to one basis with people to provide the support that they require. This gives me a tremendous freedom to respond to my clients' needs, despite how out of step these may be with other parties involved.

Although the goal of advocacy is to ensure people's voices are being heard, and not that a particular outcome is achieved, it is difficult not to feel low when an advocacy partner does not get the outcome they would like. Also, the freedom of working one to one can often be constrained by an overall demand for advocacy services. However, this is often outweighed by the enjoyment in the variety and challenge of my daily casework.

The qualities of an advocate are someone who can be assertive and strong on their partner's behalf, but has the sensitivity to empower their partner to become their own advocate. „

Margaret

Margaret is a 51 year old woman with a mild learning disability and significant physical disability. She was referred to us via a senior Social Worker who had received calls from others concerned about Margaret's vulnerability and housing support claims that she was living in far from sanitary conditions.

On meeting Margaret she presented as a fairly eloquent and aware individual, who thought she could benefit from more support – but not of the type she currently had or the type she'd had in the past...

...Margaret agreed to advocacy input to help her achieve more social work support, to help her contact welfare rights to have a benefits check and to apply for high rate mobility payments with the Department for Work and Pensions. She was also in need of better quality and more appropriate home support that recognised her efforts and limitations...

As time passed it became clear that Margaret had been inappropriately and under supported for years (and still is to some extent).

The Social Work Manager agreed to put in more support and arrange an independent living fund application. This took 6 months to materialise and to have a new care manager appointed.

Whilst introducing Margaret to the local area co-ordinator who was to work with her after advocacy input stopped, it was discovered she was struggling to pay a significant bank loan, and this was creating other debt issues. It transpired that some years previously she had applied for and been granted a loan for a man she had mistakenly trusted and relied on. She did not understand the terms of the loan, nor was she appropriately supported to consider the long-term implications and personal onus of having a bank loan. She also never saw her 'friend' again after she handed over several thousand pounds. All of this caused great concern and affected her mental health.

We met with bank staff and contacted the customer relations department who investigated the case. Eventually, the remainder of the loan was written off when it was recognised (but not admitted) that protocols and procedures to safeguard this client had not been met.

Today Margaret still keeps in touch and still finds life a bit isolating. She continues to seek friendship in the local shopping centre but is looking forward to enjoying the flexible support the independent living fund should offer her, while still retaining her independence that is so important to her.

Advocacy input has tailed off for now. However, the signs are that unless the new support package is well managed and structured to suit Margaret and her needs, there may be a re-referral in the coming months.

Being an advocate...

..."means being a voice for another person, speaking up on their behalf in situations where they feel unable to voice this. It's a vital and potent tool in the empowerment of the population."

Rik Hodgson – Positive Voice

Fiona

" I joined People First in the late 80s. I heard about it from one of the workers at a day centre that I used to go to, and thought I would see what it was like...

...When I first started going to People First meetings I didn't have the confidence to stand up and say what I thought about the things that affected my life...

...It was not long before I was encouraged by the other members to stand for the chair's job in what was then the Lothian Rights Group, and I got it.

I am now the chairperson of my local People First group in Midlothian and I am a Director on the Board of People First.

In People First groups we try to get things changed in different ways. We think change needs to happen inside people themselves. I think the groups help us to build confidence and change the way we think about ourselves.

Change also needs to happen in the way that people are seen and treated by other people. We think laws, policies and services need to change. We campaign on things like harassment, employment with a real wage, information that's accessible, hospitals closing and people having a good life in the local community in a house of their own. Over a long time, we have fought to get a voice for people with learning difficulties.

As a Director, my job is to put forward the views of our members about things that affect our lives. This could be the way we are treated by professionals, or how policies should be changed to give us the same chances in life as others...

...I have come a long way since joining People First. I would never have been able to do these things 6 years ago. In fact we never would have been asked 6 years ago...

...About 13 months ago I joined Equality 2025, the UK advisory network on disability equality. There were over 600 applicants and over 90 interviews for 21 places. As part of Equality 2025 we speak to other disabled people about what they need to lead as normal a life as possible. Then we advise the government in Westminster about what we have heard.

...If someone asked me whether they should join a People First group or not, I would say it's a good idea because the group can help them with any problems they have in their lives. You have people around you that make you feel confident whatever the decisions you have to make. You are in control. ,,

Staff at Circles Network Advocacy Project, based in the Royal Edinburgh Hospital

Breakfasting At Yours

By Jo McFarlane

Tomorrow we shall watch the steam
of your coffee pot rise
and laugh gaily amongst ourselves.
A little gathering of girlfriends
we shall be,
the shadow of womanhood
never far beneath
the veil of chitter chatter we shall wear.

When toast and marmalade are served
we shall exchange stories
of how we spent the summer:
sleeping under canvas in Mongolia;
building schools for the less fortunate
in Nairobi;
dodging bullets in El Salvador.
Or lying on a hospital bed in Morningside,
listening to Simon and Garfunkel
with thick curtains blocking out the sun.

If I make it
to your flat, that is,
and don't die of shame
on the way.

Oh Lord I am not afraid to die.
But to die like this,
being nothing,
having done nothing,
my hands not soiled with earth!

Amanda and Jane

Amanda first came into contact with mental health services when she was 17. At this point she lost contact with all her family and friends. When she was discharged from hospital she had no money and nowhere to go. She was homeless. For 9 years she battled her problems, got herself on her feet, into a flat, and got her life back. But things started to slip away again and she had to go back into hospital. This was an extremely daunting thing to happen to someone who had had such a bad experience the last time she was in hospital. Luckily, this time, Amanda met Jane. Jane is a professional advocate based in Stobhill hospital, she works with people with mental health problems on specific issues that affect their life. She attended review meetings with Amanda, making the process more bearable and understandable. Amanda is now back in her old flat, and is extremely capable. For three years, on and off, Jane and Amanda have been working together on specific problems that Amanda has come up against...

...Until Amanda met Jane she felt that she was always facing things alone. Having Jane there helped Amanda stand up for herself and empowered her to self advocate...

For one particular review meeting, Amanda's Social Worker wanted all of Amanda's health professionals to be present, which was around 10 people, all knowing about Amanda and talking about her. Amanda told the Social Worker on three occasions that she would rather have lots of smaller meetings. Amanda felt that this was an overwhelming situation to be put in and she felt that she wouldn't be able to act naturally and give an accurate impression of her recovery. Amanda called Jane and asked for help, a meeting with the Social Worker was arranged and together they convinced the Social Worker that this would not be beneficial for Amanda's case and eventually the Social Worker agreed...

...Amanda feels that this is a very typical example of how having an advocate present has helped change peoples' minds and decisions that are made about her without her input...

...A further upheaval came to Amanda's life when she learnt, on the day of her being discharged from hospital, that the building that she had been living in for 9 years was being condemned and that she had to move. Various things were not made clear like: how? when? where?...For this, Jane set up meetings with the Housing Officer, took notes for Amanda to refer back to, made sure that all of Amanda's points and concerns were addressed and acted as a witness to what was said and agreed.

Jane's job is to be impartial and work on Amanda's side. There are no ulterior motives with Jane and for this reason Amanda knew she was someone that she could trust. Having Jane there has made the difference between feeling very alone, and being able to share the battle.

Jane's funding is being cut at the end of this year, and she is the only advocate funded to work with people with mental health problems in the whole area. Who will Amanda and all of the other people Jane helps have then? No one.

For more information about advocacy and to find an advocacy organisation in your area please go to:

www.siaa.org.uk